A Story About NUMBERS

BOOK 4

Learning about numbers,
how to count to 100, and making new friends.

TTXME.com
Ten Thousand Method

WRITTEN BY
KAIWIN YEUNG

ILLUSTRATED BY
SIJARJAMIL

NUMBERS:
How many? How few?
When and where?
More or less?
Numbers help us answer
many important questions.

For free educational material
and more fun stuff
please visit our website

Special thanks to my two brothers

A Story About Numbers
Book 4 - Learning about numbers,
how to count to 100,
and making new friends.

Designed in Australia. Manufactured in China.

Written by Kaiwin Yeung.
Illustrated by Sijarjamil.

Paperback ISBN - 978-1-922978-08-0
Hardcover ISBN - 978-1-922978-09-7

NATIONAL LIBRARY OF AUSTRALIA
A catalogue record for this book is available from the National Library of Australia

Ask your local library to order a copy, so others can enjoy this book too!

A STORY ABOUT NUMBERS

BOOK 4

Learning about numbers, how to count to 100, and making new friends.

WRITTEN BY
KAIWIN YEUNG

ILLUSTRATED BY
SIJARJAMIL

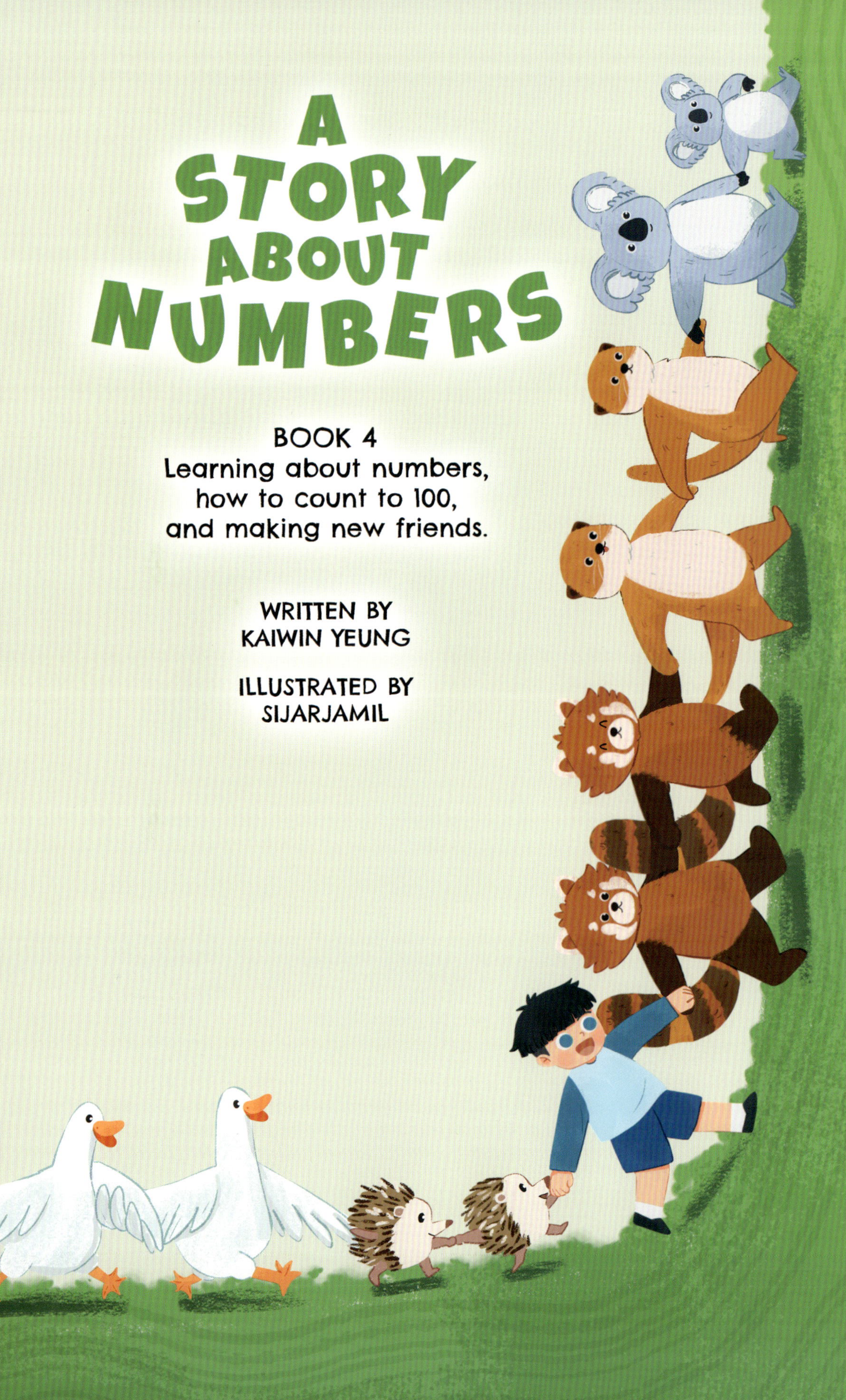

Let's have a picnic on the hill!
I'll invite my friends!

I don't have any friends.
Who can I invite?

1, 2, 3, 4, 5, 6, 7, 8, 9, 10!
10 cats!
Would you all like
to come to our picnic?

Yes! We will bring **sandwiches**!

Now I have **10 friends**
coming to our picnic.

1, 2, 3, 4, 5, 6, 7, 8, 9 and 10!
10 rabbits!
Would you all like
to come to our picnic?

Yes! We will bring **salad**!

Now I have **20 friends**
coming to our picnic.

1, 2, 3, 4, 5, 6, 7, 8
and 9, 10! **10 raccoons**!
Would you all like to come
to our picnic?

Yes! We will bring **cake**!

Now I have **30 friends**
coming to our picnic.

1, 2, 3, 4, 5, 6, 7
and 8, 9, 10! **10 foxes**!
Would you all like to come
to our picnic?

Yes! We will bring **sushi**!

Now I have **40 friends**
coming to our picnic.

1, 2, 3, 4, 5, 6
and 7, 8, 9, 10! **10 parrots**!
Would you all like to come
to our picnic?
Yes! We will bring **nuts**!
Now I have **50 friends**
coming to our picnic.

1, 2, 3, 4, 5
and 6, 7, 8, 9, 10!
10 ducks! Would you all
like to come to our picnic?

Yes! We will bring **berries**!

Now I have **60 friends**
coming to our picnic.

1, 2, 3, 4
and 5, 6, 7, 8, 9, 10!
10 hedgehogs! Would you
all like to come to our picnic?

Yes! We will bring **milkshakes**!

Now I have **70 friends**
coming to our picnic.

1, 2, 3
and 4, 5, 6, 7, 8, 9, 10!
10 red pandas! Would you
all like to come to our picnic?

Yes! We will bring **jelly** and **ice cream**!

Now I have **80 friends**
coming to our picnic.

1, 2
and 3, 4, 5, 6, 7, 8, 9, 10!
10 otters! Would you all
like to come to our picnic?

Yes! We will bring **juice**!

Now I have **90 friends**
coming to our picnic.

1
and 2, 3, 4, 5, 6, 7, 8, 9, 10!
10 koalas! Would you all
like to come to our picnic?

Yes! We will bring **pavlova**!

Now I have **100 friends**
coming to our picnic.

My friends are here!

My friends are almost here!

I have 100 new friends!
I can count them all.

We brought lots of food to share with everyone!

As numbers guide us through each of our days,
We cherish our moments in so many ways.
Come gather new friends and all bring some treats;
A picnic together is where we can meet.
We all have something to bring and to share,
A meal or a talent, or some other flair.
For when coming together, we all can see,
The beauty of friendship, in sweet harmony.

THE END...

ADDING NUMBERS UP TO 10

When Gus invites the animals to the picnic, they are arranged across the pages in numbers that equal 10, like this:
10 cats on the left page and **0** cats on the right page equals **10** cats.
5 ducks on the left page and **5** ducks on the right page equals **10** ducks.
You can read the story again or see more pairs of numbers that equal 10 here:

10+0 = 10

9+1 = 10

8+2 = 10

7+3 = 10

6+4 = 10

5+5 = 10

4+6 = 10

3+7 = 10

2+8 = 10

1+9 = 10

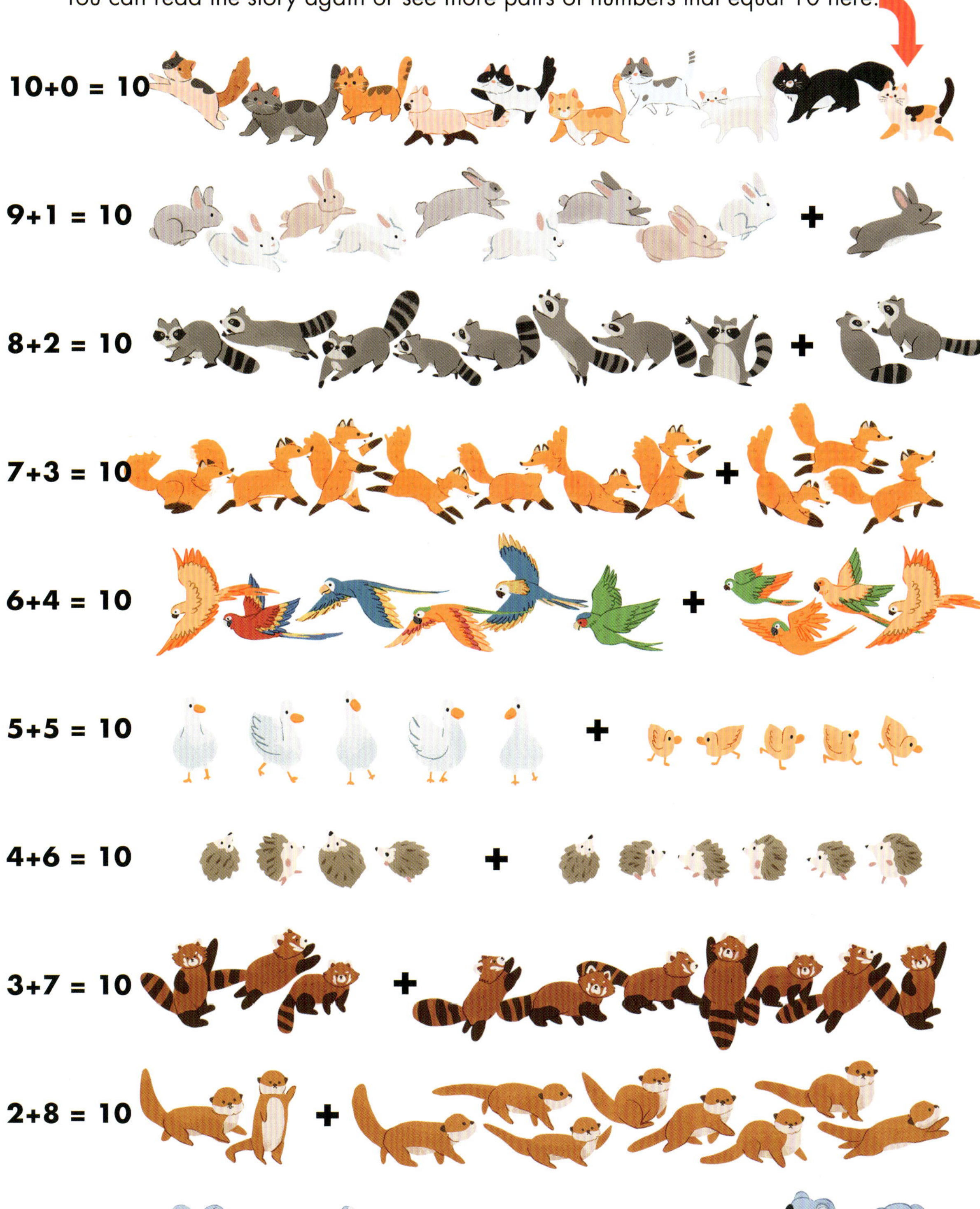

COUNTING BY 1, 2, 5, 10

You can count by **any** number, like in these examples.
Just keep adding the same number like this:

Counting by 1... 1**+1** =2 → 2**+1**=3 → 3**+1**=4 as many times as you like.

1 2 3 4 5 6 7 8 9 10...

Counting by 2... 2**+2** =4 → 4**+2**=6 → 6**+2**=8...

2 4 6 8 10 12 14 16 18 20...

Counting by 5... 5**+5** =10 → 10**+5**=15 → 15**+5**=20...

5 10 15 20 25 30 35 40 45 50...

Counting by 10... 10**+10** =20 → 20**+10**=30 → 30**+10**=40...

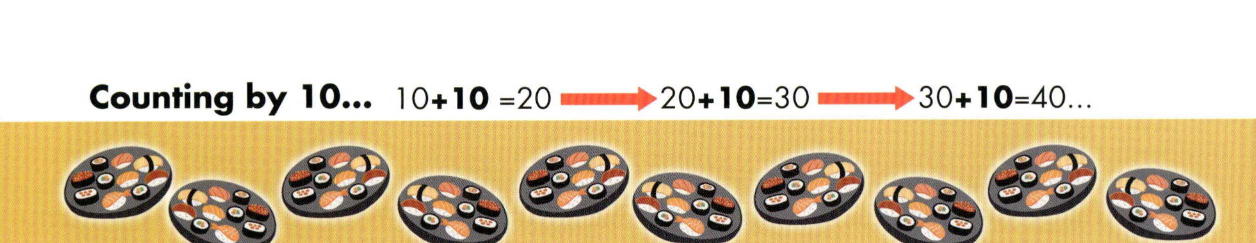

10 20 30 40 50 60 70 80 90 100...

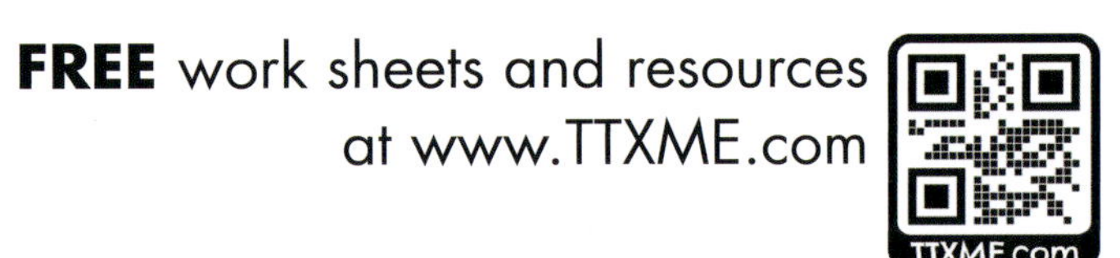

1st BOOK SERIES
Educational stories
for **early** readers
age 4 - 6.

Book 1 Book 2 Book 3

More books at
www.TTXME.com
Every book contains:

- ✅ fun story lesson
- ✅ warm messages
- ✅ pages of academic resources

Book 4